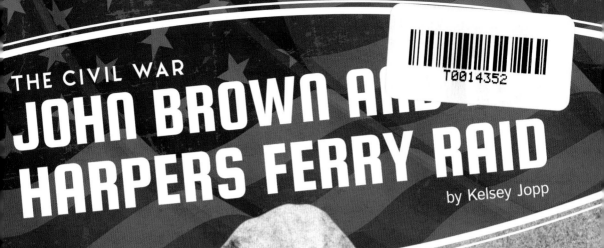

THE CIVIL WAR
JOHN BROWN AND THE HARPERS FERRY RAID

by Kelsey Jopp

T0014352

FOCUS READERS.

READERS.

VOYAGER

www.focusreaders.com

Copyright © 2020 by Focus Readers®, Lake Elmo, MN 55042. All rights reserved. No part of this book may be reproduced or utilized in any form or by any means without written permission from the publisher.

Focus Readers is distributed by North Star Editions:
sales@northstareditions.com | 888-417-0195

Produced for Focus Readers by Red Line Editorial.

Content Consultant: Dr. Gideon Mailer, Associate Professor of History, University of Minnesota Duluth

Photographs ©: Everett Historical/Shutterstock Images, cover, 1, 25, 32–33, 37; steve estvanik/
Shutterstock Images, 4–5; Ivy Close Images/Alamy, 7; AP Images, 8–9, 28; Red Line Editorial, 10, 23; John
Bachmann/Library of Congress, 12; Jon Bilous/Shutterstock Images, 14–15; Picture History/Newscom, 17,
26–27; Harvey B. Lindsley/Library of Congress, 18; Library of Congress, 20–21, 31, 35; Alexander Gardner/
Library of Congress, 39; World History Archive/Alamy, 40–41; Silas A. Holmes/Library of Congress, 43;
George Francis Schreiber/Library of Congress, 45

Library of Congress Cataloging-in-Publication Data
Names: Jopp, Kelsey, 1993- author.
Title: John Brown and the Harpers Ferry Raid / by Kelsey Jopp.
Description: Lake Elmo, MN : Focus Readers, [2020] | Series: The Civil War
   | Includes bibliographical references and index. | Audience: Grades 7-9
Identifiers: LCCN 2019031066 (print) | LCCN 2019031067 (ebook) | ISBN
   9781644930823 (hardcover) | ISBN 9781644931615 (paperback) | ISBN
   9781644933190 (pdf) | ISBN 9781644932407 (ebook)
Subjects: LCSH: Brown, John, 1800-1859--Juvenile literature. | Harpers
   Ferry (W. Va.)--History--John Brown's Raid, 1859--Juvenile literature. |
   Abolitionists--United States--Biography--Juvenile literature. |
   Antislavery movements--United States--History--Juvenile literature.
Classification: LCC E451 .J68 2020 (print) | LCC E451 (ebook) | DDC
   973.7/116092 [B]--dc23
LC record available at https://lccn.loc.gov/2019031066
LC ebook record available at https://lccn.loc.gov/2019031067

Printed in the United States of America
Mankato, MN
012020

ABOUT THE AUTHOR

Kelsey Jopp is an editor, writer, and lifelong learner. She lives in Saint Paul, Minnesota, where she enjoys practicing yoga and playing endless fetch with her sheltie, Teddy.

TABLE OF CONTENTS

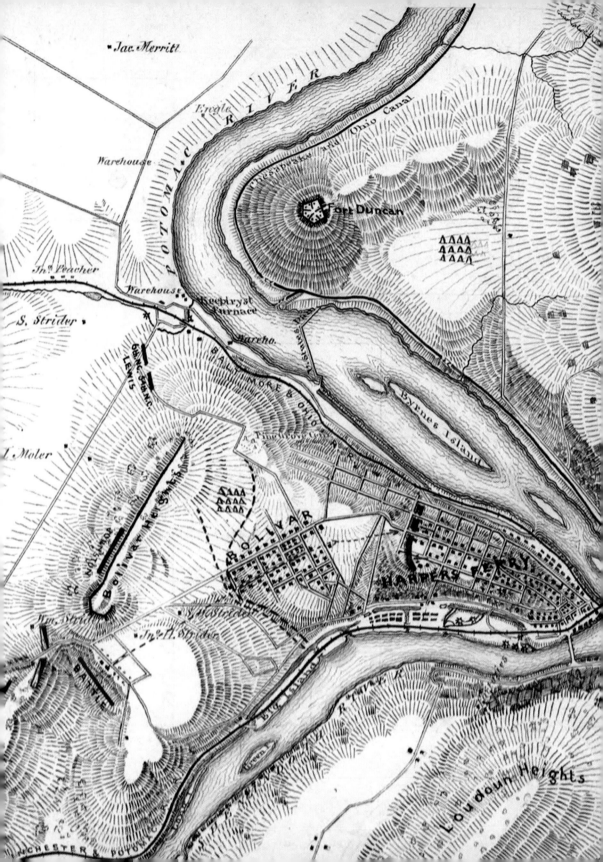

CHAPTER 1

TRAPPED

O n the night of October 17, 1859, people filled the streets of Harpers Ferry, Virginia. Despite the late hour, the entire town was awake. Only 24 hours earlier, 19 armed men had raided the small town. They captured townspeople and took control of several buildings. The leader of the raid was 59-year-old abolitionist John Brown. Abolitionists wanted to end the practice of slavery in the United States.

The town of Harpers Ferry is located along the Potomac and the Shenandoah Rivers.

At the time, slavery was legal in 15 states, including Virginia. Brown hoped his raid on Harpers Ferry would inspire an armed slave revolt. However, the raid did not go as planned. Brown thought enslaved people near the town would join the raid. This did not happen. Instead, the small group of raiders faced hundreds of soldiers and armed townspeople.

After hours of fighting, Brown and his men were trapped. Soldiers had them cornered in an engine house, a building where engines are stored. The raiders were hungry and tired. Many were wounded. Some were close to death. Brown's men pushed heavy equipment in front of the doors to keep soldiers out. But they knew they didn't have long. Eventually, the crowds outside would attack.

The US government sent troops to put an end to the raid. A group of 90 marines arrived late that

▲ Marines used a ladder to break the doors of the building where the raiders hid.

night. The next morning, they attacked the engine house with sledgehammers. But they failed to break through the building's thick doors.

Next, the marines tried using a heavy ladder. In two pushes, they made a hole in the doors. The marines stormed in, outnumbering the raiders. One marine attacked Brown with a sword. The others killed or captured the remaining raiders. Within three minutes, the attack was over.

CHAPTER 2

LEADER OF THE RAID

John Brown was born on May 9, 1800, in the state of Connecticut. His parents were very religious. John's father believed God hated slavery. As a result, the Browns became early supporters of the abolition movement.

Slavery in North America had grown quite common during the 1600s and 1700s. In 1619, Dutch settlers captured and enslaved 20 people in Africa and brought them to Jamestown, Virginia.

John Brown was an outspoken abolitionist.

They traded the African people as slaves to colonists. In the years to come, large groups of African people were forced to come to the United States through the **slave trade**. These enslaved people lived in states across the United States. However, by the early 1800s, the Northern states

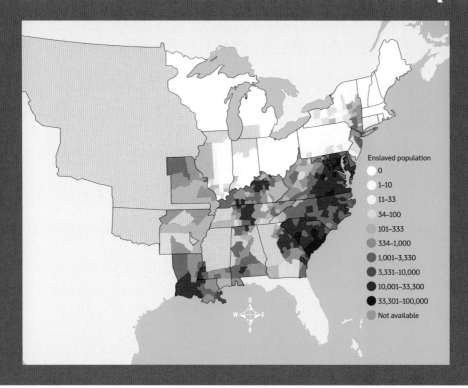

SLAVERY IN THE UNITED STATES (1820)

Enslaved population
- 0
- 1–10
- 11–33
- 34–100
- 101–333
- 334–1,000
- 1,001–3,330
- 3,331–10,000
- 10,001–33,300
- 33,301–100,000
- Not available

made slavery illegal. The remaining 15 states that allowed slavery became known as slave states.

When John was five years old, his family moved to northern Ohio. Ohio was a free state, which meant it did not allow slavery. Some people, such as the Browns, opposed slavery for religious reasons. Others felt slavery gave the South an unfair **economic** advantage. They thought free workers couldn't compete with unpaid slaves.

Some people in free states wanted to end slavery throughout the nation. As an adult, John Brown took up this cause. He participated in the Underground Railroad, a secret network of routes that people used to escape slavery. In 1851, Brown helped create the League of Gileadites. This group protected escaped slaves from being caught. Brown also developed **radical** ideas about how to end slavery.

▲ Settlers from both sides of the slavery debate rushed to the Kansas Territory in the 1850s.

In 1855, Brown settled in the Kansas Territory. One year earlier, the US Congress had passed the Kansas–Nebraska Act. This act allowed settlers in the new territories of Kansas and Nebraska to decide whether slavery should be legal there. In response, antislavery and proslavery leaders rushed to Kansas. Conflict between the two groups led to a violent uprising known as Bleeding Kansas.

Along with five of his sons, Brown fought on the antislavery side of this conflict. Like many people in the antislavery movement, Brown believed in the use of violence to end slavery. In May 1856, proslavery settlers attacked Lawrence, Kansas. This town was a major center of the antislavery movement. In response, Brown and a group of fighters led an attack on a proslavery town near Pottawatomie Creek. The group brutally killed five unarmed men. After the attack, Brown became a major figure in the antislavery movement.

After his time in Kansas, Brown turned his attention to even bigger plans. For years, he had been talking of starting a slave rebellion. He wanted to start a war against slaveholders. To make his plans a reality, Brown headed to Virginia.

THINK ABOUT IT ◁

Brown and his followers used violence to fight slavery. Do you think violence is an effective way to support a cause? Why or why not?

CHAPTER 3

PLANNING THE RAID

Brown's initial plan for the rebellion was simple. He and his followers would form a base in the Blue Ridge Mountains. These mountains ran through several states, including Virginia. Brown planned to focus his efforts in that state. Virginia had the highest slave population in the nation. Most of these enslaved people lived east of the Blue Ridge Mountains. They worked on **plantations** that grew cotton or other crops.

The Blue Ridge Mountains span 615 miles (990 km) from Pennsylvania to Georgia.

From their base in the mountains, Brown and his men would protect runaway slaves. They also planned to lead attacks on slaveholders.

In 1857, Brown shared this plan with potential supporters. He spoke with wealthy abolitionists. At the time, few abolitionists were interested in a slave rebellion. Most of them had other ideas on how to end slavery. For example, some wanted the free states to form a separate country. They were angry that President James Buchanan did not support abolition. And they didn't want to be connected to a proslavery government. However, they never acted on this plan.

When Brown met with abolitionists, he tried to convince them that violence could help their cause. He told them about his time in Kansas. Brown's stories about Bleeding Kansas were very convincing. Abolitionists raised money for his

▲ Thomas Wentworth Higginson was a member of the Secret Six. He was a Unitarian minister.

rebellion. Brown would use the money to buy land and weapons. The majority of the money came from six abolitionists. This group became known as the Secret Six.

In April 1858, Brown also reached out to Harriet Tubman. Tubman had escaped slavery in 1849. In the years after, she helped hundreds of other people escape slavery. When she and Brown met, Tubman said she respected his efforts.

▲ Harriet Tubman led more than 19 trips to help people escape from slavery in the South.

By this time, Brown's plans for the rebellion had changed. He now planned to raid Harpers Ferry. This small Virginia town held a US arsenal, which stored weapons owned by the government. Brown planned to steal the weapons from the arsenal. Then he would give them to escaped slaves. He thought this would start a war between slaves and slaveholders. Brown hoped that Tubman would join the raid, too.

Later that year, Brown was ready to act. However, one of his followers turned against him and delayed the raid for a year. In the summer of 1859, Brown was ready once again. But he had lost many followers by that time. Several of his men had changed their minds or moved away.

In August, Brown went to Frederick Douglass for support. Like Tubman, Douglass had escaped slavery and become an abolitionist. However, Douglass opposed Brown's plan. He viewed the raid as an attack on the US government, and he thought it would fail. Plus, many Northerners were against using violence to fight slavery. A raid could cause them to pull their support from the movement. Brown also lost Tubman's support, likely for the same reasons. But Brown ignored these concerns. With only 21 followers, he moved forward with his plan.

D JOHN BROWN'S RESIDENCE, KENNEDY FARM, MARYLAND.—FROM A SKETCH BY OUR OWN

lustration repre-
inasmuch that it
and execution of
Harper's Ferry

craving for glory. So far as my own experience goes, there is no
genuine love of liberty in a Frenchman. However polished he may
be in his manner and appearance, he is in heart a savage dressed in
black velvet smalls. When will my countrymen outgrow the hum-

CHAPTER 4

SURPRISE ATTACK

During the summer of 1859, Brown and his men made their last preparations. Two of Brown's sons were among his followers. The small group also included five free black men. One of these men, Shields Green, had escaped slavery and was in hiding. Others, such as Osborne P. Anderson and John Anthony Copeland Jr., had been born free. Brown worked with these free black men to plan his rebellion.

A newspaper illustration from 1859 shows Kennedy Farm, where Brown hid to plan his attack.

Brown rented Kennedy Farm as a hideout. This piece of land was only 5 miles (8.0 km) from Harpers Ferry. During the day, Brown's men hid in the farmhouse attic. They passed time by reading and playing checkers. Brown's daughter and the wife of one of his sons cooked and cleaned. They made the place seem like an ordinary farm.

To prepare for the raid, Brown studied maps. He also learned important information about the town, such as the train schedule. On the night of October 16, he finally felt ready. He gathered his men, and together they said a prayer. Then, they made their way toward Harpers Ferry. Three men stayed back to guard Brown's collection of weapons. They planned to give these weapons to enslaved people who chose to join the raid.

More than 18,000 enslaved people lived in the counties around Harpers Ferry. Brown expected

500 men to join the raid the first night. By the
next afternoon, he hoped to have 1,500 men.
Eventually, Brown planned to arm as many as
5,000 enslaved people.

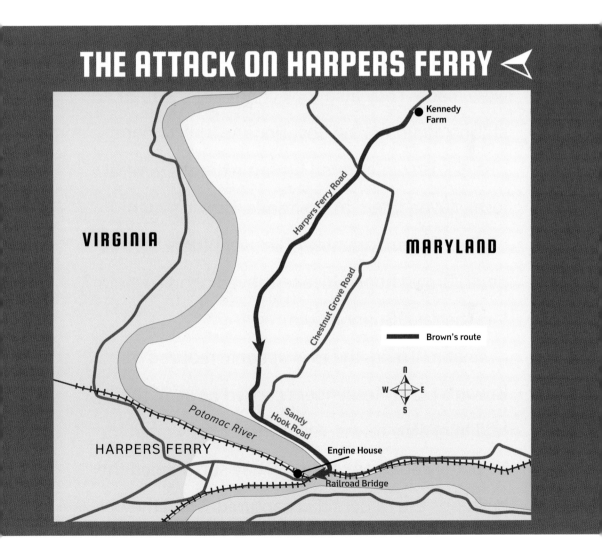

THE ATTACK ON HARPERS FERRY

Under the cover of night, the men left Kennedy Farm. They crossed the Potomac River and reached Harpers Ferry before sunrise. First, they cut the town's telegraph wires. This would prevent the town from sending for help. Then, the men captured the arsenal and armory, where weapons were made. They also took control of the railroad station and other key locations.

Next, Brown ordered his army to take several local slaveholders as **hostages**. Brown's men captured approximately 60 slaveholders. At this point, Brown hoped local enslaved people would join the raid. But none did.

That morning, the townspeople realized Brown's plan. Messengers carried news of the raid to nearby towns. As townspeople waited for help, they also took action. They surrounded the buildings the raiders had captured. Then they

Townspeople and raiders exchanged gunfire outside the armory.

began shooting. Brown's men fired back, killing the owner of the town's grocery store.

Local militias arrived around 10 o'clock in the morning. The soldiers surrounded Brown's army and cut off the escape routes. Then they shot and killed Dangerfield Newby. He was the first raider to die. Newby was a former slave. Although he had become free, his wife and children were still enslaved. He had been trying to earn money to buy their freedom.

CHAPTER 5

A LOSING BATTLE

Throughout the day, more and more militiamen arrived in Harpers Ferry. They poured in from Maryland and nearby towns in Virginia. It was clear to Brown that the raid was a disaster. Enslaved people hadn't joined as planned. The raiders were greatly outnumbered. Townspeople and militiamen surrounded the few buildings where the raiders hid. Even worse, militiamen blocked the bridge across the Potomac River.

This photo shows the entrance to the armory. The raiders took over several buildings inside.

▲ The bridge at Harpers Ferry connected the town to Maryland.

There was no way to escape. Realizing this, Brown moved into the small engine house. Several of his men and nine hostages also hid there.

At this point, Brown's best option was a **cease-fire**. He sent raider William Thompson out with a white flag. The flag meant both sides should temporarily stop fighting. That way, they could **negotiate** a deal. Brown planned to release the hostages if he and his men could go free. But his attempt at a truce failed. The angry crowd captured Thompson and held him prisoner in the local hotel.

Two hours later, Brown tried again. He sent two raiders under a second white flag. One was his 24-year-old son, Watson. This time, militiamen shot down both men. Watson crawled back to the engine house. The other raider was arrested.

Around this time, raider William Leeman escaped from the engine house. He hoped to swim across the Potomac. However, he became trapped in a narrow part of the river. When he tried to surrender, the militia shot and killed him.

THINK ABOUT IT ◁

Both times Brown sent out white flags, the other side killed or captured his men. Why do you think the militia chose to do this?

The raiders in other buildings were struggling as well. At two o'clock in the afternoon, militiamen broke into Hall's Rifle Works, which supplied weapons to the government. The three raiders hiding inside quickly escaped. They headed for the Shenandoah River, which was shallow enough to wade across.

However, the militiamen shot down two of the raiders in the water. The third man found a rock to stand on and threw down his gun. The militia accepted his surrender.

Back in the engine house, tensions were rising. Brown's men drilled holes through the doors so they could shoot at the soldiers outside. At four o'clock, one of the raiders shot and killed Harpers Ferry's mayor. Furious, the townspeople fought back. They broke into the hotel where Thompson was being held prisoner and brutally killed him.

As president, James Buchanan supported each state's right to make its own choices about slavery.

As evening approached, only four raiders remained with Brown. The rest had either escaped or been killed or captured. Both of Brown's sons died of gunshot wounds in the engine house. However, the battle wasn't over yet. That afternoon, President Buchanan had called for a company of marines. The marines planned to end the raid once and for all.

CHAPTER 6

THE END OF THE RAID

The marines arrived by train late in the night on October 17. Leading them was Lieutenant Colonel Robert E. Lee. Lee was a slaveholder. He disagreed with the abolitionist movement. He thought it made tensions between slaveholders and enslaved people worse.

When the marines arrived in Harpers Ferry, the town was out of control. Most of the townspeople and soldiers had consumed too much alcohol.

Nearly 3,400 people lived in or near the town of Harpers Ferry in 1860.

Many also had weapons and were shooting while drunk. When Lee saw this, he closed all the local bars. Next, he worked out a plan of attack. In the morning, the marines would storm the engine house. They would have to be careful not to harm the hostages inside. For this reason, they would use **bayonets** instead of rifles. That way, flying bullets wouldn't hit the hostages.

On the morning of October 18, the marines surrounded the engine house. First, they sent Lieutenant J. E. B. Stuart to the engine house doors. Stuart ordered Brown to surrender. When Brown refused, the marines made their move. They used a ladder to break through the doors and entered the building one by one.

Lieutenant Israel Greene got to Brown first. He aimed for Brown's stomach with his sword. Brown fell down, but he wasn't hurt. The sword had hit

In 1861, J. E. B. Stuart became a general in the Confederate States Army.

his belt buckle and bent in half. Thinking quickly, Greene hit Brown's head with the handle of the sword. Brown was knocked unconscious.

Just like that, the raid was over. The marines killed or captured all of the remaining raiders.

The hostages inside the engine house were left unharmed.

One week later, Brown went on trial. He and the other raiders faced charges of murder, **treason**, and starting a slave rebellion. They could be sentenced to death.

During and after the trial, Brown made several statements. He said he did not regret his actions. He believed more than ever that only violence could put an end to slavery. He had known he would likely die for the cause. In the end, he was right. A jury declared him guilty, and Brown was executed on December 2, 1859.

> ## ➤ THINK ABOUT IT

Brown's raid did not go as he had planned. What do you think he could have done differently? Could he have made the raid a success? Why or why not?

▲ Brown lay on a cot during his trial, as he had not yet recovered from his injuries.

Of Brown's small army, only five men had escaped the raid. They moved north, finding safety in Ohio and Canada. In addition to the fallen raiders, four townspeople had died. And more than a dozen soldiers were wounded. Compared to the battles that would occur in the years ahead, these **casualty** numbers were low. But this small raid had a big impact. News of the raid and trial drew the attention of the nation.

JOHN WILKES BOOTH

As a leading abolitionist, Brown had both fans and enemies. Many people had mixed views about him. For example, John Wilkes Booth both admired and hated Brown. At the time of the raid, Booth was a young actor. He was also involved in politics. Booth believed that black people were inferior to white people. For this reason, he supported slavery.

Booth belonged to a militia that was present at the Harpers Ferry raid. Booth wasn't at the raid, but he did attend Brown's execution. "When I aided in the capture and execution of John Brown . . . I was proud," Booth wrote. "I was helping our common country to perform an act of justice."[1]

Despite disagreeing with Brown's ideas, Booth called him "a brave old man."[2] He also compared Brown to President Abraham Lincoln. Both men worked to end slavery. Booth thought Lincoln was

 John Wilkes Booth was an actor. He shot President Abraham Lincoln in April 1865.

sneaky and secretive. But he respected Brown. He said, "Open force is holier than hidden craft."[3] Booth appreciated that Brown openly fought for the cause he supported.

In 1865, six years after the raid, Booth killed Lincoln. Some people wonder if he had been inspired by Brown. Like Brown, Booth chose to use violence for a cause he believed in.

1. John Wilkes Booth. *Right or Wrong, God Judge Me.* Edited by John Rhodehamel and Louise Taper. Urbana, IL: University of Illinois Press, 1997. 148.
2. Booth. *Right or Wrong.* 130.
3. Booth. *Right or Wrong.* 60.

CHAPTER 7

THE WAR AHEAD

As news of the raid spread, Brown became a **controversial** figure. Many abolitionists thought he was a hero. They admired his courage to die for a cause he believed in. However, other people hated Brown. Slaveholders disliked him because of his views against slavery. Other people agreed that slavery was wrong, but they did not like Brown's methods. They thought he was a violent madman.

Soon after Brown's death, magazines began to publish stories about his life.

The US Civil War (1861–1865) broke out a year and a half after the raid. Many historians think the raid helped bring on the war. Before the raid, the nation was divided on the topic of slavery. But many politicians and citizens thought they might be able to resolve the issue without war.

The raid made the divide worse. People on both sides of the issue grew firmer in their beliefs. For many, a peaceful resolution no longer seemed possible. Slaveholders feared that a slave rebellion might break out. In preparation, they trained and formed armies.

Participants on both sides of the raid later fought in the Civil War. Osborne P. Anderson served as a recruitment officer for the Union. And Robert E. Lee became commander of the Confederate States Army, which fought the United States Army.

The arsenal at Harpers Ferry was attacked again in the fall of 1862.

John Brown's name sparked debates for years after his death. Political leaders, activists, military members, and citizens all differed on the best methods of fighting injustice. Even today, people disagree on whether violence can fight evil. By learning from the past, they try to take actions for a better future.

FREDERICK DOUGLASS

Frederick Douglass and John Brown met in Massachusetts in 1847. At the meeting, Brown explained his plans for a rebellion. Douglass was impressed by Brown's devotion. Brown believed there was "no better use for his life than to lay it down for the slave,"[1] Douglass wrote.

After the meeting, the two men became good friends. They supported each other's efforts against slavery. However, Douglass did not approve of Brown's plan to attack Harpers Ferry. He called it "a perfect steel trap," warning Brown that "once in he would never get out alive."[2]

But in the end, Douglass had great respect for Brown. In 1881, Douglass made a speech at a college in Harpers Ferry. He spoke about the raid that had occurred more than 20 years earlier. He acknowledged that Brown's raid had failed to start a rebellion.

Frederick Douglass was one of the most prominent abolitionists in the 1800s.

"Did John Brown draw his sword against slavery and thereby lose his life in vain?" Douglass asked. "To this I answer ten thousand times, no! No man fails, or can fail, who so grandly gives himself and all he has to a righteous cause."[3] For Douglass, Brown's bravery and selflessness made him a man to remember.

1. Frederick Douglass. *Life and Times of Frederick Douglass, Written by Himself.* Hartford, CT: Park Publishing, 1881. 281.
2. Douglass. *Life and Times.* 324.
3. Frederick Douglass. *John Brown: An Address.* Dover, NH: Morning Star Job Printing House, 1881. 28.

JOHN BROWN AND THE HARPERS FERRY RAID

Write your answers on a separate piece of paper.

1. Write a paragraph that describes the main ideas of Chapter 3.

2. Do you agree with John Brown's decision to raid Harpers Ferry? Why or why not?

3. How many of Brown's men escaped to safety during the raid?

    A. four
    B. five
    C. nine

4. Why did John Brown choose Harpers Ferry for his raid?

    A. Brown had many enemies who lived in Harpers Ferry.
    B. Brown thought the white townspeople would join the raid.
    C. The arsenal held weapons that Brown could use to wage war.

Answer key on page 48.

GLOSSARY

bayonets
Long, sharp blades that can be attached to the ends of rifles.

casualty
A person who is killed, wounded, or missing in battle.

cease-fire
An agreement between opposing forces to temporarily stop fighting.

controversial
Likely to be argued about.

economic
Relating to the distribution of goods, services, and money.

hostages
People held as prisoners to force a person or group to meet certain demands.

negotiate
To reach an agreement by discussion.

plantations
Large farms where crops such as cotton, sugar, or tobacco are grown.

radical
Extreme or different from what is normal.

slave trade
The practice of buying and selling people as slaves.

treason
A crime where a person betrays his or her country.

TO LEARN MORE

BOOKS

Bolden, Tonya. *Facing Frederick: The Life of Frederick Douglass, a Monumental American Man*. New York: Abrams Books for Young Readers, 2017.

Capek, Michael. *Causes of the Civil War*. Minneapolis: Abdo Publishing, 2017.

Morretta, Alison. *John Brown: Armed Abolitionist*. New York: Cavendish Square, 2019.

NOTE TO EDUCATORS

Visit **www.focusreaders.com** to find lesson plans, activities, links, and other resources related to this title.

INDEX

Answer Key: 1. Answers will vary; **2.** Answers will vary; **3.** B; **4.** C